LAST CHANCE TO SAVE | ENDANGERED PLANTS

ANITA GANERI

PowerKiDS press

Published in 2018 by **The Rosen Publishing Group, Inc.**
29 East 21st Street, New York, NY 10010

CATALOGING-IN-PUBLICATION DATA
Names: Ganeri, Anita.
Title: Endangered plants / Anita Ganeri.
Description: New York : PowerKids Press, 2018. | Series: Last chance to save | Includes index,
   glossary, and map.
Identifiers: ISBN 9781538323885 (pbk.) | ISBN 9781538322888 (library bound) |
   ISBN 9781508162735 (6 pack)
Subjects: LCSH: Endangered plants--Juvenile literature. | Plant conservation--Juvenile literature.
Classification: LCC QK86.A1 G36 2018 | DDC 581.6'32--dc23

Editor: Sarah Silver
Designer: Alessandro Minoggi

Picture credits: Amazon Images/Alamy: 8–9. AP/PAI: 11bl, 20c. Junko Barker/Dreamstime: 3bl,
16. Stéphane Bidouze/Dreamstime: 23tl. John Bill/Shutterstock: 4b. C Kaiser–Bunbury: 17c.
Geoff Derrin/CC Wikimedia Commons: 29bl. Mikhail Dudarev/Shutterstock: 3cl, 14. ecophoto/
Dreamstime: 21l. El Viejo Cactus, Las Pilas, Matztitlan Canyon Reserve: 3tl, 13. Jonathan Esper/
Dreamstime: 3cr, 3br, 18b, 19b. feather collector/Shutterstock: 27tr. florapix/Alamy: 24t. Peter
Fodor/Shutterstock: front cover tr. Fotosearch/Superstock: 8bl. Bernard Gagnon/CC Wikimedia
Commons: 1. guichaoua/Alamy: 11br. jayeshpatil912/CC wikimedia Commons: 8cr. Christer
Johansson/CC Wikimedia Commons: 10, 20tl. Kira Kaplinski/Dreamstime: 22–23 bg. Andrey_
Kuzmin/Shutterstock: front cover br. Frans Lanting/FLPA: 15c, 23bl. Chien Lee/FLPA: 6–7, 7t.
Walter Linsenmaier/NG/Getty Images: 28r. Llama vista/Dreamstime: 18–19. Jeff de Longe/CC
Wikimedia Commons: 5b. Neil Lucas/Nature PL: 26. Alexander Mazurkevich/Shutterstock: front
cover bl. Vladimir Melnik/Shutterstock: 12. Dave Montreuil/Shutterstock: 14br. Andrey Nekrasov/
Alamy: 24c. Tim Rich: 25t. Jan Roode/istockphoto: 21cr. scarlet sails/istockphoto: 27bl. sittiitap/
Shutterstock: 4–5bg. Nico Smit/Dreamstime: 28. Christian Vinces/Shutterstock: 9tr. Ya'axche
Conservation Trust: 9bl. Tan Kian Yong/Dreamstime: 5t. Martin Zima/Dreamstime: 25c.

Every attempt has been made to clear copyright. Should there be any inadvertent omission,
please apply to the Publisher for rectification.

Manufactured in the United States of America
CPSIA Compliance Information: Batch BW18PK: For Further Information contact Rosen Publishing, New York, New York at 1-800-237-9932.

CONTENTS

ON THE EDGE

Around the world, tens of thousands of species of plants — from towering trees to tiny orchids — are in danger of disappearing for good. They are threatened by habitat destruction, illegal collecting by plant hunters, and competition with introduced species. Many are found in remote parts of the planet, and some have only recently been discovered by scientists.

The rosy periwinkle from Madagascar contains chemicals that can be used to fight some types of cancer.

PRECIOUS PLANTS

A huge variety of plants live all over the world — in the wild, in gardens, and on farms. Without them, human beings and other animals would not be able to live on Earth. Plants provide food and release oxygen that animals need to breathe. Plants can also be used as fuel, materials for clothing and construction, and ingredients in vital medicines.

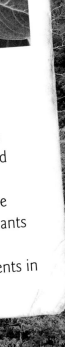

FALLING FORESTS

One of the places where plants are most at risk is in tropical rainforests. Rainforest trees are being cut down at an alarming rate for their valuable timber and to clear land for farming. About half of all species of plants and animals live in rainforests, and many are already extinct. Rainforests also soak up huge amounts of carbon dioxide, one of the gases that causes global warming, so they are vitally important to the future of our planet.

Deforestation is happening in rainforests around the world.

Thousands of seeds, like these from a Ravenala plant in Madagascar, are held at the Millennium Seed Bank.

SAVING SEEDS

Seeds from many endangered species of plants are being stored safely in botanical gardens. This means that scientists will be able to grow them in the future, even if they become extinct in the wild. The world leader is the Millennium Seed Bank at Kew Gardens in London, UK. It aims to have seeds from a quarter of the world's plants by 2020 — that's around 75,000 species.

ATTENBOROUGH'S PITCHER PLANT
(Nepenthes attenboroughii)

Attenborough's pitcher plant only grows in one place in the world — the slopes of Mount Victoria, in a remote part of the Philippines. Discovered in 2007, the plant was named after British natural history broadcaster, David Attenborough. Today, there are only a few hundred left.

MEAT-EATING PLANT

Pitcher plants are meat eaters. Their leaves form large, bell-shaped "pitchers" with slippery rims. Animals slide into the pitchers, where their bodies are dissolved by the liquid inside. Attenborough's pitcher plant has a very large pitcher — big enough to fit a hand inside — that can trap large insects and even small rodents, such as shrews.

STATS

LOCATION: MOUNT VICTORIA, PHILIPPINES

NUMBERS REMAINING IN THE WILD: 300–500

THREATENED BY: REMOTE LOCATION, PLANT COLLECTORS

UNDER THREAT

Attenborough's pitcher plant was discovered by a team of British botanists. They were told about it by two missionaries who were climbing Mount Victoria. The botanists found the new plant close to the summit. During the expedition, they also discovered another type of pitcher plant that had not been seen in the wild for 100 years.

Attenborough's pitcher plants grow on the misty slopes of Mount Victoria.

PLANT POACHING

The main threat facing Attenborough's pitcher plant is plant collecting. Despite their isolated location, pitcher plants are regularly taken from the wild and grown in greenhouses. They can be sold for a very high price. Because the plants only live in such a small area, and grow very slowly, taking even a few plants causes numbers to decline sharply. There are also plans for nickel mining on the mountain, which would put the plants' habitat at risk.

URGENT ACTION

Today, many pitcher plants are in danger. To help conserve them, botanist Steward McPherson has set up an organization called Ark of Life. McPherson is one of the botanists who discovered Attenborough's pitcher plant. Working with botanical gardens around the world, the goal is to establish collections, or "arks," of the rarest pitcher plants, in case they disappear completely in the wild.

BIG-LEAF MAHOGANY
(Swietenia macrophylla)

One of the tallest trees in the Central and South American rainforests, the big-leaf mahogany can grow up to 197 feet (60 m) tall. It gets its name from its huge leaves. The big-leaf mahogany grows slowly and lives for a long time — up to 350 years!

The big-leaf mahogany's leaves can grow over 20 inches (50 cm) long.

TOP TIMBER

For hundreds of years, the big-leaf mahogany has been highly prized for its beautiful red wood. This is used to make furniture, boats, and musical instruments. The timber trade brings vital income to the countries where the mahogany grows. But so many trees are being cut down, often illegally, that the species could become extinct in just five years.

STATS

LOCATION: Central and South America

NUMBERS REMAINING IN THE WILD: Unknown

THREATENED BY: Over-harvesting

FOREST DESTRUCTION

The big-leaf mahogany plays an important part in the forest ecosystem. When it is cut down, it sets off a domino effect of problems. The trees' roots help to bind the soil together. When they are gone, the soil is eroded and washes into nearby rivers. This damages the river habitat of many animals, including the endangered giant otter (right).

PROTECTED TREES

Since 2003, the big-leaf mahogany has been included on Appendix II of CITES (The United Nations Convention on International Trade in Endangered Species of Wild Fauna and Flora). CITES is an agreement between governments to make sure that trade does not threaten the survival of endangered species. Trade in the trees' timber is carefully controlled and permits are needed to sell it abroad.

URGENT ACTION

The Global Trees Campaign is an international program dedicated to saving the world's most endangered trees. It is working with local conservationists in Belize to try to save the big-leaf mahogany and other threatened species. Teams of rangers (such as the one above) are being trained to identify and monitor the trees, and a tree nursery has been set up in Belize.

CAFÉ MARRON

(Ramosmania rodriguesii)

In 1979, a teacher on the island of Rodrigues, in the Indian Ocean, sent his class out to search for unusual plants. He was amazed when one of his pupils returned with a cutting from a café marron plant. This wild coffee plant was thought to have been extinct for more than 40 years.

WILD COFFEE

Only a single specimen of the plant was left. It was found growing by a dusty road and had been half eaten by goats. Urgent action was needed to save it. Cuttings were quickly sent to Kew Gardens in London, UK, and the plant's identity was confirmed. Fences were put up to protect it and to stop local people from collecting its leaves and bark.

The café marron has sweet-smelling flowers that start off greenish yellow, then turn pure white.

TAT

LOCATION: Rodrigues Island, Mauritius

NUMBERS REMAINING IN WILD: 1

THREATENED BY: Grazing goats and pigs, habitat loss

Carlos Magdalena, an endangered-plant specialist at Kew, worked to pollinate the flowers.

Goats are one of the main farm animals on the island.

WIPED OUT

The café marron once grew in the island's tropical rainforests. But its numbers were devastated by grazing goats and pigs, and habitat loss. Now, the last surviving plant faced another threat. Seeing that the plant was getting so much attention, local people thought that it must have special properties. They began to collect its leaves and bark for making tea that was believed to cure illnesses.

URGENT ACTION

At Kew, botanists managed to grow a new plant from the Rodrigues cuttings. But they could not get the flowers to produce seeds. The problem was that the flowers from one café marron plant cannot pollinate flowers from the same plant. Eventually, the botanists worked out a way of pollinating the flowers and the plant produced its first fruit and seeds. Since then, several seeds have germinated. Some seedlings and seeds have been sent to Rodrigues where they will be planted back into the wild.

DRAGON'S BLOOD TREE

(Dracaena cinnabari)

The extraordinary dragon's blood tree is found only on the island of Socotra, off the coast of Yemen. It gets its name from its dark red sap, which local people use in dyes and medicines. The dragon's blood tree's unusual shape helps it to survive in its dry, rocky habitat. The monsoon brings rain, which the tree's roots soak up. They are shaded from the Sun by the tree's thick, umbrella-shaped branches, which stop the water evaporating. The umbrella also shades seedlings growing under the adult tree.

STATS

LOCATION: SOCOTRA

NUMBERS REMAINING IN THE WILD: UNKNOWN

THREATENED BY: COLLECTING OF SAP, OVERGRAZING, CLIMATE CHANGE

URGENT ACTION

The main danger facing the dragon's blood tree is climate change. Large areas of Socotra are drying out, and the monsoon is becoming less regular. By 2080, the tree's habitat could be reduced by half. Longer droughts also mean that new trees are growing without their unique umbrella shapes. The tree is protected inside the Skund Nature Sanctuary, but unless scientists can find ways of tackling climate change, its future looks bleak.

GOLF BALL CACTUS

(Mammillaria herrerae)

As its name suggests, the golf ball cactus is small, round, and white, like a golf ball. It is only found on steep mountain slopes in Querétaro, southern Mexico, in a tiny area of less than half a square mile (1 sq km). With its bright pink flowers, the cactus is a popular plant for houses and gardens. Many plants are grown in nurseries, but illegal collecting of wild plants has pushed the species to the brink. Experts think that there may be as few as 50 wild plants left.

STATS

LOCATION: Querétaro, Mexico

NUMBERS REMAINING IN WILD: around 50

THREATENED BY: Illegal plant collecting

URGENT ACTION

A conservation project has been set up in Querétaro to try to save the golf ball and four other endangered species of cacti. A greenhouse has been built to house the cacti, and local high school students have been chosen to look after the plants. They come from families who used to be involved in collecting wild cacti illegally. The idea is to educate the local community about the cacti so that they want to look after them.

GRANDIDIER'S BAOBAB
(Adansonia grandidieri)

Baobabs are known as "upside-down" trees because their branches look like roots sticking up into the air. Six of the eight species, including Grandidier's baobab, are only found on the island of Madagascar. This enormous tree once grew in forests near rivers and lakes. Today, as its natural habitat has been destroyed, it is mostly found in open farmland.

UPSIDE-DOWN TREES

The Grandidier's baobab can grow up to 98 feet (30 m) tall. It has a huge, cylindrical trunk. In times of drought, the tree stores water in its trunk, which swells in size, then shrinks as the water is used up. In the summer, the tree grows large white flowers that open at night. Lemurs, bats, and birds pollinate them.

A bird feeding on a baobab flower.

USEFUL BAOBAB

Baobabs are highly valued by local people, who use every part of the trees. They make juice from the fruit, eat the seeds, and extract oil from the seeds. The thick, reddish-gray bark is stripped from the trunk and used to make ropes and medicines. The trees are also important in local culture, as they are believed to be the homes of spirits.

The baobab tree bark is cut to make ropes.

STATS

LOCATION: MADAGASCAR

NUMBERS REMAINING IN THE WILD: AROUND 1 MILLION

THREATENED BY: LOSS OF HABITAT

HABITAT LOSS

The baobab's habitat in southwest Madagascar is under serious threat, as large areas of their forest home are being cleared for farmland. It is also threatened by fire, overgrazing of seedlings by livestock, and bark and seed collecting.

URGENT ACTION

Conservationists are trying to save Grandidier's baobab. In Madagascar, the local organization Madagasikara Voakajy (MV) is working with specially trained "tree monitors" who check the baobabs throughout the year and report any damage or deforestation. The monitors wear T-shirts printed with images of the tree to raise awareness among local people. MV has also planted 200 baobab seedlings to replace the trees lost.

JADE VINE

(Strongylodon macrobotrys)

The jade vine is a long, woody vine that grows in the rainforests of the Philippines, where it climbs around tree trunks. Today, its rainforest home is under threat, and the vine faces an uncertain future. The jade vine grows blooms of beautiful jade-green flowers that are shaped like claws. The flowers have evolved their shapes so that they can be pollinated by bats. While the bats hang upside down to drink the nectar, their heads get brushed with pollen.

STATS

LOCATION: PHILIPPINES

NUMBERS REMAINING IN THE WILD: UNKNOWN

THREATENED BY: HABITAT LOSS

URGENT ACTION

Botanists in Britain managed to grow the jade vine in nurseries, but they had trouble getting the flowers to pollinate. Then, they had a brilliant idea. They used their hands to mimic a bat's head and carried the pollen to another plant.

JELLYFISH TREE
(Medusagyne oppositifolia)

STATS

LOCATION: Seychelles

NUMBERS REMAINING IN THE WILD: Fewer than 90

THREATENED BY: Not being able to produce seedlings

The very rare jellyfish tree grows on the island of Mahé, in the Seychelles. It grows up to 33 feet (10 m) tall, and gets its name from its small, white flowers, which look like jellyfish tentacles. Botanists are mystified by the jellyfish tree. Its seeds do not seem to be able to germinate in the wild, and there are no new, young plants being produced. Botanists have successfully grown seedlings in nurseries, but the seedlings have only grown in very humid conditions, which are not found in the tree's natural habitat.

URGENT ACTION

The jellyfish tree was declared extinct in 1930, but 40 years later, six trees were discovered. Today, there are about 86 jellyfish trees left in the wild. These are protected in the Morne Seychellois National Park, a huge area in the center of Mahé island.

MONKEY PUZZLE TREE

(Araucaria araucana)

The monkey puzzle tree is an evergreen conifer from Chile and Argentina. It mainly grows in forests on the lower slopes of the Andes Mountains. The tree has spiky branches that are covered in spiny leaves, and it can grow 164 feet (50 m) tall! It was given its name because people thought that climbing the spiky branches would be a puzzle, even for a monkey!

USEFUL TREE

The monkey puzzle is the national tree of Chile and the symbol of its national parks. It is also important for local people. They eat its seeds, roasted or boiled, which are said to taste like chestnuts. They also grind them into flour and use them to feed their livestock in winter. Wood is used for fuel and building.

The cones drop to the ground, so they are easy to collect — no climbing is required!

TAT

LOCATION: Chile, Argentina

NUMBERS REMAINING IN THE WILD: Unknown

THREATS: Fire, Logging, Grazing

GARDEN FAVORITE

Thanks to their striking appearance, monkey puzzle trees are popular in parks and gardens. In the early 20th century, thousands were planted in Europe and North America to show off people's wealth. In the wild, though, their natural habitat is under serious threat.

FIRE HAZARD

Monkey puzzle trees grow in volcanic areas, where there is a risk of wildfires breaking out. Because of its features, such as thick bark, the trees tend to grow back well. But more fires are being started to clear land for farming. Huge areas of the forest have been burned, damaging large numbers of trees and destroying their habitat.

In Chile, many trees are being protected in reserves.

URGENT ACTION

The International Conifer Conservation Program was set up in 1991 to protect the world's endangered conifers. In partnership with Rainforest Concern, it purchased a patch of forest in Chile to set up as a nature reserve. The main trees in the reserve are ancient monkey puzzle trees (the species can live for more than 1,300 years). There are plans to buy more forest in the future in order to expand the reserve.

PYGMY WATER LILY

(Nymphaea thermarum)

The pygmy water lily is the world's smallest water lily. It is also one of the world's rarest plants — there are no pygmy water lilies left in the wild. The water lily was discovered growing around a hot spring in Rwanda in 1987. The spring was fed by water from an underground aquifer. Local farmers began using the aquifer for water to irrigate their fields. This cut off the supply to the spring, and the water lily's fragile habitat dried up.

The pygmy water lily has tiny, green pads, each only about the size of a fingernail!

STATS

LOCATION: RWANDA

NUMBERS REMAINING IN THE WILD: NONE

THREATENED BY: LOSS OF HABITAT

URGENT ACTION

Luckily, botanists at Kew Gardens in London were able to grow the pygmy water lily from cuttings saved before it became extinct. They did this by copying its unusual living conditions — most water lilies live in water, but this plant lives in damp mud. There are now more than 50 plants growing at Kew, and a small number in Germany.

QUIVER TREE
(Aloe dichotoma)

The striking quiver tree grows in the dry, rocky deserts of South Africa and Namibia. It is an important tree in its habitat. Its bright yellow flowers attract large numbers of insects and birds, such as sugarbirds, for pollination. The local San people use its branches to make quivers for their hunting arrows. The greatest threat to the quiver tree is climate change. Experts predict that the tree's habitat is likely to get hotter and drier, and the quiver tree may struggle to adapt. Huge numbers of the trees have already died off because of drought.

A bird feeding on the flowers of a quiver tree.

STATS

LOCATION: South Africa, Namibia

NUMBERS REMAINING IN WILD: Unknown

THREATENED BY: Climate Change

URGENT ACTION

In response to the dangers of climate change, botanists in South Africa are looking at planting groups of quiver trees in places outside their current range. They hope that the climate in these places will be more suitable for the trees' survival.

21

RAFFLESIA

(Rafflesia arnoldii)

With no leaves or roots, the rafflesia is a highly unusual plant. It grows inside woody vines in the rainforest and, for most of the time, cannot be seen at all. Then a bud bursts through the bark and the rafflesia's extraordinary flower starts to bloom.

SUPER-SIZED FLOWER

A rafflesia flower can grow up to 3 feet (1 m) across, making it the largest single flower of any plant. It has five large, fleshy, reddish-brown petals covered with pale spots. The flowers smell of rotten meat, which attracts flies to pollinate them. It takes around 10 months for a bud to grow into a flower that blooms for just a few days.

STATS

LOCATION: Southeast Asia

NUMBERS IN THE WILD: Unknown

THREATENED BY: Habitat loss, tourism

UNDER THREAT

The rafflesia faces many threats. Logging is destroying its rainforest habitat. Local people collect flower buds for use in traditional medicines. There are also dangers from the plant's own life cycle. New buds often die — only around 10 percent go on to bloom.

A rafflesia flower bud.

TOURIST TRAP

Thanks to its amazing flowers, the rafflesia has become a tourist attraction, and many people come to see it bloom. This brings an income for local people who act as guides, but it is also putting the rafflesia at risk. Careless visitors trample the vines that the rafflesia grows in, and, as a result, there are few buds being produced each year.

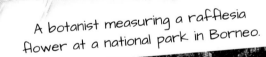

A botanist measuring a rafflesia flower at a national park in Borneo.

URGENT ACTION

The rafflesia are protected in a number of nature reserves, including the Rafflesia Forest Reserve on Borneo. But much more needs to be done. Some of these reserves are not well looked after, and the plants are damaged or dead. In particular, conservationists are hoping to involve local people in the care of the plants.

23

SINAI PRIMROSE

(Primula boveana)

This small plant only lives on the slopes of Mount Sinai in Egypt. It has rosettes of grayish-green, spear-shaped leaves, and golden-yellow flowers. With fewer than 200 left in the wild, the Sinai primrose's future is looking uncertain. The primrose grows in moist ground and relies on regular, light rainfall. But, as a result of climate change, both droughts and floods are increasing, putting its habitat at risk. Local people also need the precious water for drinking and farming, and insect pests eat the plants.

STATS

LOCATION: EGYPT

NUMBERS IN THE WILD: FEWER THAN 200

THREATENED BY: CLIMATE CHANGE, HABITAT LOSS, INSECT PESTS

URGENT ACTION

All of the remaining wild Sinai primroses are found inside the St. Katherine Protectorate, an Egyptian national park (above). Most are protected by fenced enclosures, and regularly monitored by park rangers. Tens of thousands of people visit the park each year. The rangers check for any damage to the plants and their habitat from these tourists.

SNOWDONIA HAWKWEED

(Hieracium snowdoniense)

There is only one surviving Snowdonia hawkweed plant left in the wild. It grows on a steep, rocky mountain cliff in Wales. The plant was thought to be extinct for years, but it was rediscovered in 2002. Over the last 50 years, there has been a huge rise in the number of sheep grazing in the Welsh mountains. The sheep may have grazed the Snowdonia hawkweed almost to extinction. Now, any chance event, such as a rock fall, could wipe the whole species out in the wild.

Grazing sheep have pushed the hawkweed to the brink.

STATS

LOCATION: WALES, UK

NUMBERS IN THE WILD: 1

THREATENED BY: OVERGRAZING

URGENT ACTION

The Snowdonia hawkweed's habitat has been protected as a Site of Special Scientific Interest and sheep are no longer allowed to graze nearby. It is hoped that this will help the plant's numbers to recover. Seedlings have also been grown in the National Botanic Garden of Wales, which may be put back into the wild one day.

25

TITAN ARUM
(Amorphophallus titanum)

With its huge leaves and giant flowers, the titan arum is one of the strangest-looking plants in the world. It grows on steep hillsides in the rainforests of western Sumatra, Indonesia. It is also grown in nurseries and botanical gardens, where it is a popular attraction with visitors.

FREAKY FLOWER

The titan arum is famous for its massive flower that can grow up to 10 feet (3 m). The flower only opens for 48 hours and gives off a terrible smell to attract insects, such as beetles and flies, for pollination. When the flower dies back, the plant grows a huge, single leaf as tall as a small tree.

FOREST LOSS

The titan arum's natural habitat is being destroyed at a rapid pace. Vast areas of the rainforest have been cut down for timber or to clear space for oil palm plantations. Indonesia has already lost around two thirds of its forests, and the destruction is continuing at a rapid pace.

The rhinoceros hornbill is vital for scattering the titan arum's seeds.

TAT

LOCATION: SUMATRA

NUMBERS REMAINING IN WILD: UNKNOWN

THREATENED BY: LOSS OF HABITAT

PRECIOUS PLANT

Loss of habitat affects the titan arum directly, but it also puts other species in danger. These include the rhinoceros hornbill, which relies on the plant for food. There are other reasons for saving this lily. Scientists are carrying out research to see if the plant could be used to treat sleeping sickness, which kills thousands of people in Africa each year.

The giant flower is a popular attraction at botanical gardens, like this one in New York.

URGENT ACTION

Botanical gardens around the world have been working hard to find ways of growing the titan arum. This has not been easy. Even under ideal conditions, a titan arum may take 7–9 years to flower! They are also tricky to re-pot. The plants grow from corms, or underground stems, that can weigh more than 154 pounds (70 kg). The tallest flower so far reached 10 feet (3 m) tall and was grown in New Hampshire.

WELWITSCHIA

(Welwitschia mirabilis)

The welwitschia, or tree tumbo, is found in the Namib Desert. It is well adapted to its harsh habitat. Its two leaves soak up moisture from the sea fogs that roll over the desert. The leaves can grow up to 13 feet (4 m) long, becoming torn and frayed by the wind and weather.

The welwitschia grows very slowly and lives for a long time — some plants may be over 1,000 years old. But a fungus that attacks the plant's cones and seeds is quickly becoming a cause for alarm. The fungus causes the seeds to rot and die soon after they have germinated.

STATS

LOCATION: Namibia, Angola

NUMBERS REMAINING IN THE WILD: Several thousand

THREATENED BY: Fungus, plant collecting, damage by vehicles

URGENT ACTION

Many welwitschia are protected inside national parks, and scientists monitor them regularly. Recently, a group of plants were dug up and moved out of the way of a new road that was being built in a mining area.

WESTERN UNDERGROUND ORCHID

(Rhizanthella gardneri)

This unusual orchid spends its whole life underground. It has a white stem that produces clusters of tiny dark red flowers. Underground insects, such as termites, pollinate the flowers. The orchid feeds on fungi that live on the roots of broom bushes. The orchid is only found in Western Australia, where fewer than 50 are left in the wild. Large areas of its bush habitat have been turned into farmland. Drought is another serious threat.

There has also been a loss of the broom bushes on which the orchid depends for food.

STATS

LOCATION: WESTERN AUSTRALIA

NUMBERS REMAINING IN THE WILD: FEWER THAN 50

THREATENED BY: DROUGHT, HABITAT LOSS

URGENT ACTION

Botanists in Australia are working to safeguard the orchid's future. The wild plants are protected inside nature reserves. A collection of seeds has also been saved and stored, so that new plants can be grown in nurseries. This is in case the orchid becomes extinct in the wild.

GLOSSARY

AQUIFER
A section of rock that can contain or carry water underground.

BOTANICAL GARDEN
A garden that is dedicated to collecting, growing and displaying a wide range of plants.

BOTANIST
A scientist who studies plants.

BROADCASTER
Someone who talks on radio or television programs.

CACTUS
A spiny plant that grows in deserts in North, Central, and South America.

CLIMATE CHANGE
A change in the climate of the world, largely caused by the increase in the world's temperature.

CONIFER
A tree, such as a fir or pine, that grows cones and spiky, evergreen leaves.

CONSERVATIONIST
A person who works to protect the natural world and its wildlife.

CORM
The thick, swollen, underground stem of some plants.

CUTTING
Part of a plant, such as a stem or leaf, that grows into a new plant.

CYLINDRICAL
Shaped like a cylinder.

DEFORESTATION
Cutting or burning trees down in an area.

DROUGHT
A long period of dry weather, with no or little rain.

ERODE
Wear away, by water or the weather.

EVAPORATE
When liquid water turns into water vapor (gas).

EVOLVE
How a plant or animal species changes over time.

GERMINATE
When a plant's seeds sprout and grow into new plants.

GLOBAL WARMING
An increase in the world's temperature, caused by carbon dioxide and other greenhouse gases in the atmosphere.

GRAZING
Grass and plants that are available for animals to feed on.

HUMID
Moist, damp weather caused by water vapor in the air.

IRRIGATE
Bring water from a river or lake to water a farmer's fields.

LIVESTOCK
Animals, such as cattle and sheep, kept on farms or ranches.

MISSIONARY
Religious person who travels abroad to teach people about their beliefs.

MONSOON
Winds blowing across Asia that bring heavy rains.

NECTAR
A sweet, syrupy liquid found inside flowers.

NICKEL
A soft, strong, silvery-white metal.

OIL PALM
A type of palm tree with fruits that produce palm oil.

PEST
An animal that damages plants and crops.

POLLINATE
To take pollen from one flower to another, or from one part of a flower to another, so that a seed can grow and form a new plant.

ROSETTE
A pattern that looks like the petals of a rose.

SEEDLING
A very young plant that has grown from a seed.

TERMITE
A tiny insect.

LOCATION MAP

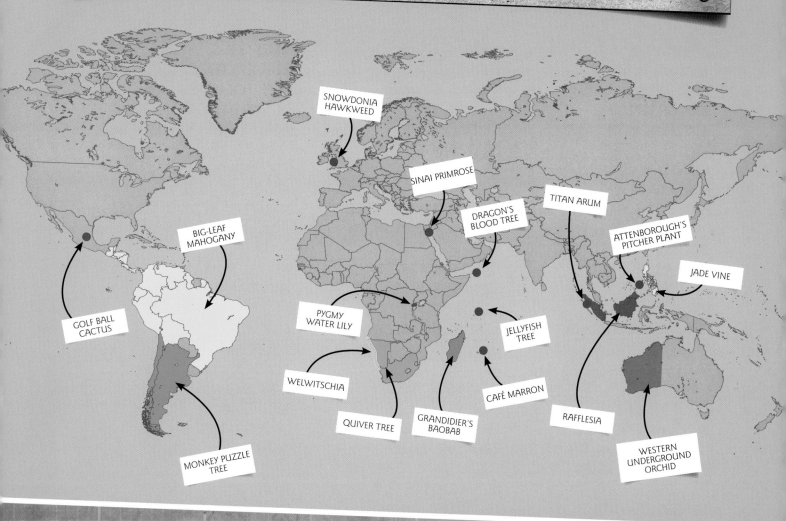

SNOWDONIA HAWKWEED

SINAI PRIMROSE

TITAN ARUM

DRAGON'S BLOOD TREE

BIG-LEAF MAHOGANY

ATTENBOROUGH'S PITCHER PLANT

JADE VINE

GOLF BALL CACTUS

PYGMY WATER LILY

JELLYFISH TREE

WELWITSCHIA

CAFÉ MARRON

QUIVER TREE

GRANDIDIER'S BAOBAB

RAFFLESIA

MONKEY PUZZLE TREE

WESTERN UNDERGROUND ORCHID

FURTHER INFORMATION

PowerKids Press has developed an online list of websites related to the subject of this book. This site is updated regularly. Please use this link to access the list:

www.powerkidslinks.com/lcts/plants

INDEX